First edition

Published in the United States by Strong Arm Press

Images based on photography by Rebecca Sive.

Design by Paige Kelly and Jenna Floricel Lewinstein.

First Printing: January 2022

Make Herstory Your Story

Subjects: Women In Politics; Political Advocacy; Success Self-Help

For information about bulk orders, contact Strong Arm Press.

Credit to Hayley Gilmore for the poster image, A Woman's Place is in the Resistance, used with permission.

Printed in the United States of America.

ISBN: 978-1-947492-58-5

MAKE
HERSTORY
YOUR STORY

YOUR GUIDED JOURNAL
TO JUSTICE EVERY DAY
FOR EVERY WOMAN

REBECCA SIVE

STRONG
ARM
PRESS

"We are fighting for an unapologetic moment for economic, social and racial justice in the United States."

The Hon. Alexandria Ocasio-Cortez, "AOC"
Member, U.S. House of Representatives

"I want to be remembered as someone who used herself and anything she could touch to work for justice and freedom...I want to be remembered as one who tried."

Dorothy Height, Leader, 1963 March on Washington, President, National Council of Negro Women

"Every moment is an organizing opportunity, every person a potential activist, every minute a chance to change the world."

Dolores Huerta, Organizer
Founder of the National Farm Workers Association, women's rights leader, farmworker

Herstory is...

The story of women told from an explicitly feminist perspective. It is the collective account of millions of women everywhere, including you, who advocate justice and equality for every woman and girl—by leading campaigns, organizations, and projects; by creating inspirational works of art; and by demonstrating through their own accomplishments that there are no limits to what women and girls can accomplish. Herstory is every woman's story; the story of every woman and girl who has cared and made a difference for the better.

"Make Herstory Your Story made me recall the phrase: 'women hold up half the sky.' *Make Herstory Your Story* makes this communal commitment of ours a joy to imagine and an achievable dream."

Sol Flores

Deputy Governor, State of Illinois,J.B. Pritzker, Governor

"Make Herstory Your Story is an easily accessible book full of musings, reflections, and summaries of inspirational actions that empower women. The journal encourages readers to define themselves, write their own stories, and create their own strategies for using their strengths to navigate a world that is in the midst of substantial social change."

Michelle Duster

Author, *Ida B. the Queen: The Extraordinary Life and Legacy of Ida B. Wells;* Educator, Public Historian, Great-granddaughter of Ida B. Wells

Dear Sisters:

Early in my career as a feminist organizer and social justice advocate, I was in graduate school, working on my masters' degree in American History, writing a thesis about the women who founded Hull-House, a settlement house in the heart of a Chicago immigrant neighborhood. The commitment of those inspiring women was to build a community center, together with the neighborhood's residents, to uplift and empower the community. Pacifist- and community organizer extraordinaire—Jane Addams, and her sister founders, devoted their lives to working with their neighbors to achieve this mission. They envisioned and carried-out strategies and campaigns. They dreamt big; they became independent political players (an unusual circumstance for women of that era); and they were instrumental in the creation of a more just United States. They recorded their accomplishments. They made Herstory.

Down Halsted Street, in another Chicago neighborhood, Ida B. Wells was doing the same. From time-to-time, she and Addams collaborated on national campaigns for social justice and civil rights. Just as we do together today, they worked together to dismantle racism, sexism, and the other destructive forces women and girls too often experience.

They, along with the women I've worked with in my own social justice and feminist activism, inspired me to write **Make Herstory** to help guide your creation of Your Story as Herstory. The journal is divided into three sections: imagine; create; and organize. Each section includes 15 chapters; each with an inspirational or motivational graphic (derived from my Women's March photos), accompanied by my suggestions for your thinking and journaling in that message context. Do use the messages of the graphics to motivate and inform your plans, and to encourage you to answer questions related to them. You'll find tips to help you to determine what steps to take and connections you want to make. The goal is to foster your thinking about the justice-making path you want to take, and the projects you want to create along that way. Also in the journal are pages for you to make notes about the women's organizations, movements, leaders, and activists whose Herstory-making inspire you. I can't wait to read Your Story as Herstory.

In sisterhood and with best wishes for the journey,

Rebecca Sive

September 2021

Table of Contents

"When people doubt your right to be somewhere, the responsibility falls on you to prove over and over again that you deserve to be there."

Stacey Abrams,
Strategist, Voting Rights Activist

My guided journal to making Herstory, including my story.

_____

MY NAME

_____

DATE

> "I'm not the next Usain Bolt or Michael Phelps. I'm the first Simone Biles."

Simone Biles
Olympic Gymnast

IMAGINE

Our first step in this great journey to justice for every woman begins with imagining the place you want to be at the end of your journey.

Your first step in this great journey to achieving justice for every woman and girl begins with imagining the place you want to be at the end of your journey—imagining how Your Story will read. What do I want to have achieved for myself; for other women, for girls? What are the steps I need to take to achieve this goal? Who will I need–and want–by my side as I make this journey to making Herstory? What new skills do I want to have once I've made this journey?

Let your mind run free to record your imaginings of projects, organizations, works of writing, music, art, or athleticism. Imagine the scope of the work you're committed to. Think about how Herstory–and Your Story–will fit together. Then make some notes here. Since there are fifteen inspirational chapters here, you can imagine lots of projects! Some tips for imagining Your Story as Herstory for every woman:

- Sit in an inspirational space for you–inside or out–with pleasant light and in a comfortable way.

- Describe your sense of yourself in your moments of greatest creativity.

- Visualize yourself talking to a large group of women or girls about your dreams of justice for every woman and girl; then, describe how you want to make this dream come true.

- Identify the "aha" moments you imagine you will experience along the way to achieving these dreams.

- Describe the qualities of the people who you want to be by your side during this journey.

Now, time to imagine Your Story as Herstory.

Marian Wright Edelman, founder of the Children's Defense Fund, was quoted in Jennifer Siebel Newsom's documentary, *Miss Representation*, as saying: "you can't be what you can't see." In doing so, she explained why knowing our Herstory is so important. If you can see Herstory, you can make Your Story Herstory. I first saw an image expressing this idea of make Herstory–as a directive to me and every other woman who saw it–many years ago. But when I saw it on a Women's March poster presented in this bold format, it was just so compelling. I felt a part of the idea. So, imagine here the opening lines of Your Story in the Herstory books that will be written about our times. And then imagine the projects you want to create that reflect this description of Your Story.

Here are some suggestions for imagining Your Story as Herstory:

- Think about the women you admire most (whether they are famous or not)–and you find most inspirational–and write down why.

- Think about the sorts of projects you want to do, and how having the qualities of these women you admire will help you accomplish your dream projects.

- Is there a project you have in mind that you believe will be uniquely valuable to Herstory? If so, note it here.

MAKE
HER
STORY

Realizing your dreams requires being able to control your reproductive destiny, *whatever* you have decided that destiny is. When I saw this poster at the Women's March, I immediately responded to both its message, *and* the way that the words move, suggesting to me that each of us can move ourselves and others in order to make every woman free, by working to preserve her right to make her own reproductive choices. As you think about the overriding truth expressed here, and how it relates to the reproductive choices you have already made, or may be making in the future, I ask you to remember *this* truth: the fact that Herstory of the utmost importance, for example, achieving the right to vote, was made by women who didn't have the reproductive freedom that we have to make our own choices. Yet, they persevered. You will, too: importantly, collaborating with other women whose reproductive choice will be different from yours, but who also deserve the right to control their own bodies and create Herstory. Your Story always includes telling this truth: every woman has this freedom.

Imagine Your Story in a way that honors women's reproductive autonomy:

- How much more your project will mean if every woman is free to participate, unconstrained by an inability to control her reproductive choices. Describe or draw this picture.

- Are there ways you can incorporate positive messages about women's reproductive choices in the projects you're envisioning, whether or not they are related directly to this issue?

- Are there strategies for organizing women to participate in your project that work regardless of differing reproductive health choices? Think here about the fact that some of the women you will work with will have children; some will not. Some will be able to afford childcare; some will not. How will you help all these women?

NO WOMAN
CAN CALL
HERSELF FREE
WHO DOESN'T
OWN AND
CONTROL
HER BODY!

Pink and silver glitter on this poster caught my eye, spelling out a powerful message, displayed triumphantly and carried proudly through the streets of downtown Chicago by an African American woman and girl. Like the message in the prior chapter about your right to control your body, I think Your Story as Herstory always encompasses this idea, too: misogyny has no place anywhere. And, if you see it, you will also say: "chill." Unfortunately, the reality of misogyny is that—left un-chilled—it knows no constraints. It can survive in any atmosphere; it can be experienced by women and girls of any age. Whether Your Story as Herstory will be made in the country or the city; on the plains, or in the mountains; on a farm or in an apartment building, you will need to be ready to confront and chill the misogyny around you. You can do it: here are some tips.

Remember, and be prepared to deal with this truth, that even usually fair-minded people may have misogynistic thoughts. How will you chill them?

- What are your responsive tactics for calling-out misogyny that don't deter you from imagining Your Story as Herstory?

- If you have to just move on, don't be afraid to do so: Your Story means you control your moves. How will you do this in the context of imagining your projects?

- As you imagine your particular justice-making projects, what are the ways in which you can generally promote the idea of "chill with that misogyny"?

CHILL WITH THAT MISOGYNY

I know you see those vigorously-raised hands, just as I did on this marvelous poster, which was carried by two teenage girls with very big smiles. I imagine you're raising your hand, too, as you imagine how to use your outside voice to create Your Story as Herstory. Speaking of raising your hand, some of you here will remember being afraid to raise your hand in school. The way I heard it was that the girls were supposed to let the boys (only) raise their hands to speak with outside voices. Well, I heard that and said "no." If you haven't yet, you can, too. And, if using your outside voice feels scary or intimidating, consider this: no doubt, you would use your outside voice to get help for a person you cared about, who was in trouble and needed help. Well, all of us need help these days! One way or another. And that outside voice can make that truth clear. Also, remember that helping–using your outside voice to further justice–means you care. And that caring will mean using your outside voice as often as is needed.

When you think about using your outside voice in order to imagine a Herstory project, think about these truths:

- The louder you speak, the more people will hear you— and, therefore, the more people will be able to consider what you have to say and even join your project. What do you most want to shout to the rooftops about your project?

- Using your outside voice is a good way to quickly gather others around you who also care deeply about the project you're imagining. It tells them you value your work. What are the words you most want to shout out?

- Does thinking about using your outside voice conjure up an image of yourself you value? If so, how about drawing that image here, or gluing in here a photograph of yourself?

It is Time to use our OUTSIDE VOICES

One of our greatest and constant opportunities is to be able to express ourselves freely–in speech *and* in writing–thanks to the *First Amendment to the US Constitution*: "Congress shall make no law respecting an establishment of religion, or prohibiting the free exercise thereof; or abridging the freedom of speech, or of the press; or the right of the people peaceably to assemble, and to petition the Government for a redress of grievances." However, as you probably have experienced, perhaps when speaking too hastily, how you say those words matters. As this poster reads: "words matter," both those that are chosen, and then how they are expressed. In this context, I often remember this important truth: you never know what difficulties someone may be going through when you speak to them; so, never speak harshly. Words matter. No need, ever, for that mode when making Your Story as Herstory. Instead–when making Your Story as Herstory–the words that matter most are inspirational *and* concrete. Speaking this way will motivate others to join you to make Herstory.

When I'm imagining my Your Story as Herstory projects, I find myself googling for just the right words to express the idea I've imagined. I can then jot them down for ongoing reference. What words matter most to you in this context?

- How will you use these favorite words to describe the project(s) you're imagining?

- An important part of telling Your Story as Herstory is using words that aren't gender-linked. So, for instance, you will want to say, or write: here is how I will "staff" my project, versus here is how I will "man" it. (This advice may seem obvious to you, but it's just amazing to me how frequently this form of sexism, not to say misogyny, turns-up. What's your response to those who criticize you for being too politically-correct?)

WORDS
MATTER

I know some women don't like to read or hear the word "girl" to describe an adult woman, even in jest or in slang. But, to me, using "girl" connotes energy and optimism, just how most girls are. And I love describing my women friends as "girlfriends." It brings them closer to me, even if only metaphorically. It's clear to me that the girl who carried this Women's March poster was energized to share this idea with *girls of all ages*, as she marched down the street with hundreds of thousands of other "girls," of every age. Then, there's the word "fight": well, as a community organizer, making Your Story as Herstory, sometimes you will just have to fight for what you believe in to make this Herstory come true. There is just nothing the matter with that degree of passion for justice-making. To me, the concept of "fight like a girl" is like the idea that you can never care too much about something. If that requires a fight, so be it.

Think about "fight like a girl," as a needed part of the projects you are imagining:

- To fight doesn't mean to literally exchange blows, or even to raise your voice. It does mean using your outside voice to make your point. (The one that reads: I care. A lot.) What sorts of circumstances create in you a desire to fight? Are there ways to avoid those circumstances and still get to imagine your project being successful?

- Jot down some words here you prefer to use when you're mad—whether talking or corresponding with those who disagree with your dream of Your Story as Herstory.

- When you feel so strongly that you are prepared to fight, think about and note here the words you always want to say to your opponent about your hope that the two of you will find a way to agree.

Fight Like A Girl

Okay, girlfriends: this image expresses one of my all-time favorite feminist messages. While the dictionary defines "deflower" as "depriv[ing] a woman of her virginity," as Tony Soprano would say: "forget about it." This incredibly sexist definition takes away a decision that is *women's alone* to make (unless she is the victim of rape). Necessarily, the message on this poster–seen on posters in many women's marches and other women's protests across the country–pushes that definition aside. Instead, it is the patriarchy that needs to be deprived; deprived so much so that it withers and dies like a flower at season's end. As a gardener myself, I have also found analogies to gardening useful to my political messaging and organizing. For instance, in both gardening and politics, we are growing something valuable. Further, in both contexts, we tell a story by what we grow and nurture. I have no doubt that Your Story will grow as you deflower the patriarchy.

Describe here the images that come to your mind as you grow and nurture your projects to create Your Story as Herstory.

- What are aspects of matriarchy that fit with your images of your projects?

- What do your descriptions here tell you about what you're willing to accept or, alternatively, confront and deflower, as you create Your Story?

IMAGINE DATE: / /

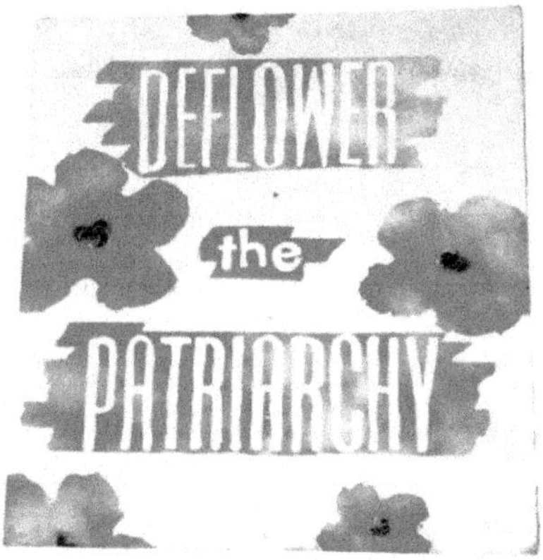

Almost 250 years ago, Olympe de Gouges wrote the *Declaration of the Rights of Woman.* In it, she states: "[Men] what gave you the sovereign right to oppress my sex?" Fifty years ago, the United Nations declared: "Women's rights are human rights. Attaining equality between women and men and eliminating all forms of discrimination against women are human rights." While women of the world could, and do, unite for myriad reasons, uniting to champion equality is clearly the implication of *this* declaration. And since equality once achieved can take many different forms, e.g., equal pay, equal voting rights, equal access to healthcare, a question for you is this one: how will you champion women uniting in your projects that are Your Story as Herstory?

Think here about how the projects you're imagining, and how the messages and activities they will embody can support a universal campaign for women's unity.

- Now, imagine your role in this universal women's campaign: how will you choose to be a part of it, and what do you want to contribute?

- Dreams like uniting all women can be modeled in your own community of girlfriends. How does that look and feel to you?

WOMEN
OF THE
WORLD

UNITE!

Can you imagine Herstory has her eyes on you and all women and girls? I think the creator of this poster, marching for justice with tens of thousands of other women and girls, imagined it ought to. I agree with her. She suggests here that we have a communal obligation to gift equality and justice to the generations of women and girls to come. And to inspire them to create Herstory, too. As this communal dream motivates your journaling, remember just how much those future generations will want to know Your Story. How did you accomplish what you did? What impelled you to be a part of making Herstory? How did you encourage other women to join you in making Herstory?

Imagine your projects as living forever, and what it will take from you to create the possibility of that longevity.

- Some women dream of fame as well as leadership and accomplishment. If that's a dream of yours, too, record here your thoughts on how you will realize this dream.

- What are the words that will best describe how you want future generations to describe Your Story?

DATE: /   /

HISTORY
HAS ITS
EYES ON
ALL OF US

The Women's Marches held the day after President Trump was inaugurated were motivated by the deeply-rooted anger of women everywhere who understood that the US had just elected as POTUS a racist and sexist; a person to resist. Today, while Donald Trump is no longer POTUS, his horrific legacy continues to hurt far too many women, tragically including those who continue to believe in him and his message. (Why: you ask. Well, that's a story for another day!) Fortunately, those of us dismayed at the dismantling of American freedoms Trump generated remain committed to an US in which there truly is "liberty and justice for all." Imagining and writing Your Story as Herstory is one way to realize this dream. While you do, remember that–regardless of race, ethnicity, political perspective, or even class–commonly, we experience sexism and, consequently, benefit from resisting together.

- Imagine your project as a catalyst for women resisting together in order to create a better world for women and girls. How do you describe it?

- As you think about the importance of resisting, what are the words or images that you want to share with the women in your life who you want to join you?

- How do you imagine talking with like-minded women of other races, classes, or experiences about the importance of working together? What words and images come to mind here?

RACIST
SEXIST
FASCIST
RESIST

I'm not wild about using the term "pussy," but I admit it is useful when visualizing—and even describing—justice-making projects to think of them in the most vivid context you can. The words "pussy" and "grab" certainly do that! I've even heard them in serious conversations among feminist activists to underscore the importance and positive impact of angry women organizing for women's rights. When I saw this poster, I saw the pretty writing of the word "pussy." Clearly, that imagery was important to the woman who created this poster. Does "pussy" in pretty pink connote something in particular for you?

- Imagine and note here the kind of project you think about creating that could be described as a "pussy grabs back" one.

- What are your thoughts about the use of seemingly pejorative slang expressions to describe women coming together to do something positive? Does that resonate for you, or does the idea of it feel bad?

- In light of the campaigns by anti-reproductive-choice activists, do you see value in couching your imagined projects in the context of slang describing women's bodies?

THIS
Pussy Grabs Back

I have always liked women's art images that draw your attention to their key words. This is certainly one (and with exclamation points besides): "DONE...QUIET!!!" If you've been quiet, too, and are now ready to bust out and are journaling Your Story here, take this poster-maker's words to heart. Imagine as you do the sorts of projects you want to create that will engage lots of other people, who are also ready to bust out. And as you do, remember this old-timey adage: "If a tree falls in a forest and no one is around to hear it, does it make a sound?" Likewise, you'll want to gather around others as you dream and create. Does it matter if you are so soft-spoken that others have to strain to hear you? Yes, it does. But note that I don't mean screaming or yelling here: I do mean imagining ways to share your project widely through the descriptive power and loud volume of your words, so even those not attuned will hear them and be compelled to listen carefully and respond.

- How do I imagine myself when I'm done being quiet? Happy, sad, boisterous, with others? If so, with whom; doing what?

- I'm done with this—I've completed this; whatever it is that now gives you the time to make Your Story. Describe.

- When I'm in a quiet space, can I still imagine making Herstory? If so, does it feel any different? Yes, and I differently describe it here.

I am DONE
being
Quiet !!!

Sixty-five million plus American voters chose HER. Women were the majority of those voters. Since then, I've met many women who still feel that day was one that changed their consciousness—forever. They express their feelings–and commitment to greater political activism on behalf of women–in all-capital-letters, too. I'm with HER, too. That all-caps feeling feels exactly right to me, too. Had you asked me, even just a few years before 2016, whether I could have imagined voting for HER to hold the most powerful job in the world, I would have said "not hardly!" And then to experience her loss to someone of such low character; so much less well-qualified; so much less suited by virtue of his work experience, education, and personal behaviors. Truthfully, in 2021, the mind still boggles. But I feel good knowing I voted for HER, and that I got the chance to do so again in 2020. And someday a woman *will* be president.

- Imagine how you felt when you voted for HER. Write those words down or draw that image of your face. Then, think about how those feelings relate to Your Story.

- Did you imagine what you most wanted HER to do once she was elected? Write down those ideas or plans and see how they may relate to Your Story as Herstory.

- If you were whispering in HER ear in the Oval Office, imagine and describe here the project you would whisper about first. And, if it's your project, how do you start telling Your Story to her?

❚❚ Fired up and ready to go" is how the entire phrase
goes for those of us who heard Barack Obama when
he was first campaigning to be POTUS. This poster in the
2017 Women's March was quite literal: its colors were
fiery orange and red. You sure couldn't miss the concept.
Everything about the image made me feel like joining *that*
fired-up woman. I also realized that I had been fired-up
back in the 2008 Democratic primary season when I fully
reflected on the idea that a woman or an African American
man might be POTUS. And then, once again, in 2020 when I
reflected on the idea that while I had been fired-up in 2012
about electing our first African American POTUS, and in 2018
that one of the Democratic women campaigning to be the
POTUS nominee might prevail. I was once again fired-up in
2020 when Kamala Harris became the first African American
woman nominated for the vice-presidency and the first
woman to win it. The phrase "yes, *she* can" jumped to mind.

- How do you imagine yourself when you're "fired-up"?
  Is there something telling when you are, which will
  energize you for the projects you imagine, for making
  Your Story?

- In your mind, is there anything negative about being
  "fired-up"? Any fear of being perceived as bossy, or of
  being called a bitch? Or anything else?

- Imagining projects to organize as Your Story as
  Herstory, which one makes you the most fired-up?

_____

_____

_____

_____

_____

_____

_____

_____

_____

_____

_____

_____

_____

_____

_____

_____

_____

The earliest reference to the term "fempire" I've found was describing a self-named group of women screenwriters. Along came a song, a tee-shirt, Women's March posters from all over the place portraying this message, even a beer! *This* version was carried in the Chicago 2017 Women's March. A man and a woman marched together: the woman held this sign. Ironically, the man carried a poster, too, about women in power. It proclaimed: "Who runs the world?" Consider the irony when you consider the lyrics to Beyoncé's *Run the World (Girls)*: "My persuasion/Can build a nation/Endless power/With our love we can devour." Yes: that's the mantra of the fempire, which will enable women to run whatever else they want. For this poster's creator, and for me, too, women running the world means peace—see that peace symbol there? What a lovely idea.

- Do you imagine Your Story as part of a fempire?

- For this bold vision, what sorts of women will be your first recruits?

- Will you strike back peacefully if attacked?

THE
FEMPIRE
STRIKES
BACK

My description of the project I've imagined:

_____

_____

_____

_____

_____

_____

_____

_____

_____

_____

_____

_____

_____

_____

CREATE

Now that you've imagined
Your Story as Herstory,
you're ready to create those
ideas by describing them
in this section of your
journal. To create, describe
your projects in as great a
detail as you can.

Here's an example for you from my journal: one of my dreams is to create a community center for the women and girls who live in my neighborhood. So, in this journal section of mine, I'm sketching-out this concept. Like you, I'm using the graphics and messages here

to inspire my journaling. I'm also going to describe here as many of the other projects I've imagined as I can. You could do the same thing. I recommend waiting till the mood strikes you, and you have some quiet time to yourself. Also, you might think about placing your project descriptions in the chapter here with the most connected message. For instance: if you want to organize a women's reproductive health project, you might want to create it on the page: "My uterus, my opinion." You can also take the messages in the graphics as inspiration for more than one project idea. For instance, Beyoncé's idea noted here: "Okay ladies, now let's get in formation" is an all-encompassing idea for Your Story as Herstory!

So, to create each project idea you've imagined, go ahead and record in this section of your journal the answers to as many of these questions as you can:

- Why is the project needed?

- What the essence of the project is; what are its primary activities; what is its scope—for instance, is it local, regional, national, or even international?

- Who will be involved?

- Who will be helped?

- When is the best time for you to launch, considering both your capacity and the network you have built, as well as external circumstances like elections?

This image isn't elegant, but it is compelling. Considered in the context of creating projects benefiting women and girls, the image affirms two important truths for every woman: your autonomy *in body and in mind*, and your right to do what you imagine, unconstrained by those who would push you down. Since these two truths are foundational to creating Your Story, keep them front and center in your mind. Also, as you journal and create, remember that the expression, "don't tread on me," was first used on a flag during the American Revolution to portray the revolutionaries' goal of achieving freedom from royal, male tyranny. That's what you are doing, too: achieving freedom and justice for all women. You may also want to create a flag–or a poster like this marcher did–proclaiming these truths for yourself.

- If you imagined Your Story as a project related to women's reproductive autonomy and health, what are the elements of it?

- Alternatively, if you imagined a project advancing and preserving women's freedom from tyranny, what are its elements?

my uterus,
my opinion

DON'T TREAD
ON ME

❚❚Build bridges, not walls." While this idea is simply stated, its implications are profound. For instance, were you building a bridge or a wall, a lot of thought—and a lot of resources—would need to go into it, in order to make sure it's safe. Likewise, the metaphorical building of a wall or a bridge requires significant thought and resources and a concern, say, for the safety of those who meet on the bridge. The creator of this image also implies that it's most fruitful to build as many bridges as you can, and as few walls as possible. You know this from other experiences of becoming. Walling-out others means little access to them and little opportunity to gather together in common cause. It's also true that walling-out others can creates enemies while building a bridge so you can talk, but you (still) disagree, probably won't.

Here, you've committed to Your Story as Herstory as engaging with others as much as you can. If you build a bridge and can even only meet in the middle, that's so much better than no meeting at all; no chance to further your dialogue in the future; no opportunity to recruit others who share your view of Herstory.

- As you record here how you want to create one of your projects for Your Story as Herstory, record here also your preferred ways to build bridges to a common understanding with those who need to be convinced of the merits of your plans.

- Are there projects you've imagined that are essentially bridge-building initiatives? If so, what are your strategies for, metaphorically-speaking, building those bridges as long and wide as possible?

BUILD

not

And SHE is with you. Remember this truth as you are imagining and creating your projects. HER essence—to be yours—is expressed in the Emma Lazarus poem on a bronze plaque inside the Statue: "Here at our sea-washed, sunset gates shall stand...A mighty woman with a torch.... From her beacon-hand...Glows world-wide welcome." You get the idea: SHE, whose essence is liberty and justice for every woman and girl, symbolizes and affirms our right—and our duty—to our sisters to secure equality for every one of us. The contemporary slogan, "I'm with her," was created by a graphic designer for Hillary Clinton's presidential campaign. As you no doubt know, it quickly became a popular phrase in many feminist contexts. When the designer was asked about the feelings she wanted the slogan to elicit, she said her goal was to be "accessible, ownable and about inclusion." That's your goal here, too, as you create Your Story as Herstory and, thus, are with HER, too.

- How will your project creation embody and exemplify the spirit of "I'm with HER"?

- Does the word "SHE" have particularly important qualities you want expressed by the women who join you in making Herstory?

I'M WITH HER!

Ihave friends who recite empowering mantras every morning as they prepare for the day. One is: "not afraid." Their belief in the importance of this approach to life stems from their belief that every woman and girl has *the right to not be afraid.* Not afraid of the threat of sexual violence, or of any other kind of violence, as she creates her world and Herstory. To me, it follows that because every woman has *the right* to not be afraid, she should have the right to not be afraid in her public work, however different from the commonplace. This isn't to say that you won't experience moments of trepidation as you create Your Story. Those are to be expected; they are natural occurrences when beginning anything new and important. So, proceed not afraid, building bridges not walls.

- As you are journaling here, think about what you do when you have a bad dream. You could record those actions here, so you remember as you go forward in this aspect of your becoming.

- If you have well-founded fears due to something you experienced in the past, or even continue to experience, record here some of your strategies for getting past those fears so you can deploy them as you engage in creating Your Story.

Not
Afraid

It is so interesting to me that encouraging women to "think again" was so forcefully portrayed in a poster carried at a march for women's rights. Typically, such parades' posters make declarations about "women's issues," for example, about reproductive rights, or equal pay, or the need for affordable childcare. However, in this case, the poster-maker created a flag in red, white, and blue, exhorting marchers to "think again," implying a past when Americans thought more wisely than they do today. However, in the 19th century, ignorance abounded, too. There was actually a political party named the Know-Nothing Party. It was nativist, anti-immigrant, and anti-Catholic, trafficking in conspiracies about non-Protestants supposedly attempting to undo American constitutional freedoms. Those people weren't thinking straight either, just as those who happily inaugurated Donald Trump the day before I saw this poster were not. Had they, they would have realized that their racist, sexist, and anti-immigrant beliefs aren't thoughtful–or right–either. Some of them would even have you believe that wearing a mask to protect the spread of a disease is the same limitation on personal freedom as the experience of Jews and others in the Holocaust. So, it's still time to make America think again—but with concern, love, and a commitment to equality.

- How will your Herstory project educate those with dangerous, racist, and hateful ideas to think again–to think about how wrong those ideas are?

- What will you do if one of these hateful folks approaches you spewing hate for the people your project supports and the ideas it espouses?

MAKE
AMERICA
THINK
AGAIN

One of the most inspiring young feminists in my circle *only* dresses in 1950s-style clothes. She styles her hair in that era and wears the red lipstick women favored back in that day. She has been presenting herself this way for almost as long as she has been an active feminist. As I've gotten to know her better, I've grown to understand this passion of hers, seemingly at-odds with her powerful feminist commitment. But it's not. She's as down with fourth-wave feminism as any woman I know. None of my feminist friends is more committed to not go quietly back to homophobia (this friend is also a lesbian), or to the profoundly destructive nativism, racism, and sexism that so damaged that time in American life and destroyed the dreams and lives of so many women—and men.

- In the Donald Trump era and now continuing, the ugly racism and sexism of the 1950s has risen again. For instance, the Proud Boys feel like a contemporary version of the Ku Klux Klan, a far-right organization that promotes and sanctions political violence. And there are the adherents of QAnon. According to the *New York Times*, "QAnon is the umbrella term for a set of internet conspiracy theories that allege, falsely, that the world is run by a cabal of Satan-worshiping pedophiles. QAnon followers believe that this cabal includes top Democrats like President Joseph R. Biden Jr., Hillary Clinton, [and] Barack Obama." Last but by no means least are the anti-choice and anti-women's equality women Members and Senators who hearken back to Phyllis Schlafly and her acolytes. If the project you've imagined will require confronting these adversaries, so like those our antecedents experienced in the 1950s, how will you prepare yourself?

- Create here the argument you will make for support of your project to a woman who thinks that 1950s womanhood was just fine.

DATE: / /

I WILL NOT GO QUIETLY BACK TO THE 1950s

Repeatedly, Michelle Obama famously said that she didn't like politics. However, watching her for eight years in the White House, as well as in the years since, you've no doubt seen just how committed she is to making the world a better place—the very purpose of any political institution. I think it was the too-often ugly and fractious context in which political work is too often done that impelled Obama to remind us when she made this statement of why we should be doing political work. When I saw this poster carried by a little girl in the 2017 Chicago Women's March, I was happy for the reminder. We had just come off one of the ugliest election seasons imaginable. That little girl reminded us of the fundamental reason for marching: in order to create basic human decency for all.

- Imagine here a world in which basic human decency reigned. What will the project you're thinking about now feel like? What will it accomplish?

- Politics is just like the rest of life, in the sense that even people with common goals will differ from time-to-time on how to achieve those goals. So, political back and forth is a constant. That just can't be helped. What's important is to be clear to and for oneself about the boundaries for that back and forth, so that the goal of human decency is met. What are those boundaries for your project's creation? Are there pieces you're willing to sacrifice to create it?

It's not
about
POLITICS.
It's about
**BASIC
HUMAN
DECENCY.**
— michelle obama

Perhaps in your circle this belief goes without saying. But that's not the case in far too many places. In so many, both men and women still hold the view that the (only) way to be a woman is this traditional way: as a heterosexual, a mother, and a homemaker. This view holds even when the majority of American women work outside the home (57% of all women over the age of 16). Too often, women's paid work is considered secondary to work at home. For instance, during the lockdown due to the COVID-19 pandemic, according to the *New York Times* (5/17/2021), "5.1 million American mothers stopped working for pay." Now more than ever, as millions of women of every kind are eager to be employed once again, in positions that respect their life choices and pay equally, there is no wrong way to be a woman if every woman is to have equal opportunity and respect.

- As you create your project, record here the affirmative ways every woman will be made welcome.

- If your project is focused on girls, record here the ways in which you will teach them "there is no wrong way to be a woman," and how you will model your belief in this truth for them.

THERE IS
NO WRONG WAY
TO BE
A WOMAN

"Ally" is a noun. For instance, you are my ally. It is also a verb: I ally with you. In either case, the goal is to ally in a significant and long-lasting way. Preferably, you and I are allies with a deep emotional and political connection rooted in unshakable trust. So, if we first ally to undertake a project or champion a cause, hopefully that alliance is followed by many more.

As you create here projects to benefit women and girls, such alliances are your desired ends—both for yourself as you lead and guide and for those who join you. I promise you: your allyship among a wide and deep circle of women will then become the cornerstone of your lifetime of being uplifted by other women and their uplifting you. How magnificent will that be!

- Your Story as Herstory is dependent upon building alliances with women who share certain personal qualities. What are the personal qualities you seek (and need) in your allies to create your project?

- How do you characterize the circles of allies you want around you? Moving outwards from the center of your circle —you— in concentric circles with the closest-in being the most closely-allied, characterize your circles.

_____
_____
_____
_____
_____

_____

_____

_____

_____

_____

_____

_____

_____

_____

_____

_____

_____

_____

The woman who carried this poster looked tough. She also held her head high and marched with great energy and determination; though by herself, as though she were leading others. Her poster quoted Madonna. I knew the quote but didn't remember it was Madonna's: no surprise there! Here is another quote from Madonna that can guide your journaling here: "A lot of people are afraid to say what they want. That's why they don't get what they want." Well, as you've gotten this far in this journal, you have not only stated what you want, but begun to plan how to get it. Left unsaid by Madonna, though, is this truth: what you want; have imagined; and have created in these pages is also what other women want. They are also tough and ambitious; so totally deserving of your taking this approach. And, if you, or one of them, is called "bitch"? You'll also say I'm OKAY with that.

- Knowing what project you want to create doesn't require knowing every step along the way, but you will want to sequence the big tasks so that you can build efficiently and avoid redos. As you create your project, note here the sequence of tasks that makes the most sense to you.

- Worth recording here are some pithy come-back lines if someone calls you "a bitch," and you want to respond equally forcefully.

I'm
TOUGH,
I'm
AMBITIOUS,
and I know
EXACTLY
what I want.
If that makes
me a
BITCH,
OKAY.

Since the earliest days of the nation's Herstory, women have imagined and created projects benefiting the common good. Abolitionists like Sojourner Truth, suffragists like Alice Paul, labor organizers like Mother Jones, and community organizers like Jane Addams and Ida B. Wells, refused to be silent; refused to be stymied in their campaigns to improve women's and girls' lives; and refused to accede to temporal defeats.

This graphic is a vivid reminder of their and your commitment to keep speaking. Again, here is the text of the *First Amendment to the US Constitution*, which states that right and is the document the Statue of Liberty represents: "Congress shall make no law respecting an establishment of religion, or prohibiting the free exercise thereof; or abridging the freedom of speech, or of the press; or the right of the people peaceably to assemble, and to petition the Government for a redress of grievances."

- What is the role of speaking in creating your project? Is it to inform others, or is it also integral to the very nature of the project? Depending on your answer here, you'll need to think differently about how Your Story will read as Herstory.

- If you find patriotic images alienating, what other images would you choose to underscore your commitment to the right to free speech?

_____

_____

_____

_____

_____

_____

_____

AMERICAN
women
WILL·NOT·BE
SILENT

_____

_____

_____

_____

_____

_____

_____

_____

_____

_____

O ver the last forty years, the US economy has become progressively more unbalanced, evidenced in the fact that most of the nation's financial resources are concentrated in the hands of very few white men. "Microsoft co-founder Bill Gates, Amazon founder Jeff Bezos and Berkshire Hathaway CEO Warren Buffett have collectively more wealth than the 160 million poorest Americans, or half the population of the United States," according to CNBC in 2017. During the COVID-19 pandemic and subsequent shutdown of the American economy, tens of millions were unemployed and most had insufficient cash reserves. Millions of women lost their jobs. Mind you, half of all women workers earn less than $48,000/year and many are the sole support of their families. Pretty much all of us American women are not billionaire white men, nor anything close to that, but when it comes to creating a better world for women and girls, what we do have– determination, and smarts, and care for one another–makes up.

Two issues are at the fore here:

- Making sure the women who work with you on the project you're creating make equal pay for equal work. What are your ideas about how to make this happen?

- Making sure that the project, as you create it, takes into account how it can advocate or support campaigns that seek to decrease the wage gap between women and men and the income chasm between the rich and the rest of us, which harms so many girls and women. How can your project complement efforts to increase wage equality for American women?

WE'RE NOT
BILLIONAIRE
WHITE MEN

Perhaps you're creating a project that deals directly with the wage disparities that plague American women workers: between men and women, between white women and women of color, and the most egregious disparity—the one between white men and women of color. If so, your creativity can take many forms. It can focus on one of these problems; alternatively, it could focus on the overall problem of gender inequality. If you decide to focus on one aspect of this problem, I hope you will couch that work in the largest possible context. Remember your thought about the concept of "ally" a few pages back? Well, that's what you want to achieve here, too: allyship with every woman, for pretty much every woman has experienced wage disparity in her life as a worker. This is common ground to build on.

- There's a not-so-funny meme that goes like this: "One explanation for the gender wage gap is that men typically gravitate towards higher paying jobs like doctor, engineer, CEO...while women tend to gravitate towards lower paying jobs like female doctor, female engineer and female CEO." As you create your project here, make sure you and any women you hire aren't caught in this trap.

- Perhaps, you're creating a project for girls that focuses on their future work life. How can you create it to share the truth of systemic discrimination against women while staying optimistic about the possibility of their achieving their professional dreams?

DATE: /   /

Fix WAGE Disparity

American Herstory is rife with incidents of too much hate and too little love. African American suffragists were asked by their white peers to walk at the back of the suffrage marches. While the 19th Amendment granting federal suffrage to American women was ratified in 1920, it wasn't until passage of the 1965 Voting Rights Act, which rendered illegal state and local barriers to their voting, that African Americans were more freely able to vote. Today, racist policymakers continue to advocate voter suppression, which makes it imperative for all of us to advocate for the idea that love, not hate, makes America great.

- The biblical command, "love thy neighbor as thyself," can be applied here as you create your project. How can your project foster love, as it helps or advocates?

- If your project is an artistic one–a painting, or a musical composition, or a textile, or a sculpture, say–do you want to carry this message forth in it?

- If your project is an athletic achievement (think Simone Biles) that will demonstrate there are no physical limits to what women and girls can accomplish, how can it manifest love for one another?

Love not HATE makes AMERICA Great

" Cause I slay. I just might be a Black Bill Gates in the making…Okay, ladies, now let's get in formation." And there you have it: direction from Beyoncé to imagine and create at as large a scale as you can imagine. Perhaps, like her, conceptually as big a project as Bill Gates created, but, unlike him, in formation with as many of your sisters as possible. A young, African American woman carried this poster, which so cleverly combines imagery that bespeaks Black Power and women's power. I also saw these words on other posters when I photographed the 2017 Chicago Women's March. Time to get down with all of those women and Beyoncé.

- Beyoncé's video, titled "Formation," is rich in cultural images related to the Herstory of African American women. She also ties this Herstory to what she hopes to achieve in formation with other women. As you create, consider how you can do the same with your project.

- If your project is an artistic one, primarily one built alone—say, a painting, or a musical composition, or a textile or a sculpture—how can you still embody the idea of being in formation with other women?

_____

_____

_____

_____

_____

_____

_____

_____

_____

_____

_____

_____

_____

_____

_____

_____

_____

_____

My description of the project I've created:

_____

_____

_____

_____

_____

_____

_____

_____

_____

_____

_____

_____

_____

_____

_____

ORGANIZE

Congratulations on reaching this stage of your journey of justice-making for every woman and girl, creating Your Story as Herstory.

N ow, here is my guidance for approaching this part of making Your Story. To begin, I want to tell you a story about Barack Obama. Remember when Barack Obama announced that he wanted to be POTUS? Perhaps you realized when you heard his announcement that he

must have imagined this goal many years before; and that, to have a chance at success, that he must have made his plan for achieving this dream many years before, too. How else you'd wonder, could he have stood up to the world so boldly and confidently?

While President Obama didn't have *this* journal to guide him, he likely journaled, too. First: he imagined being POTUS. Second: he created his path forward, answering his who, what, when, where, and why questions. Finally, he was in his organizing phase; just as you are now. Here are some of the questions he likely answered: What is the sequence of my organizing activities; what is my primary message; how can I win early on so I demonstrate the viability of my idea; what's my response to those who question my qualifications for doing *my* project (being POTUS)?

Now, it's your turn to record the organizing plans for *your* project. Again, use the messages in the graphics here to motivate and inform your plans and to help you think through important issues related to them. On the next page, I've shared some pointers for how you'll make Your Story Herstory.

Remember how I told you I wanted to create a neighborhood women's center? So, using that example as a prototype for yourself, below are some of the questions I'm answering and recording in my *Make Herstory* journal. They can guide building Your Story, too. And, if you're an artist, or a writer, or a musician, or an athlete, and that work is Your Story as Herstory project, you will still want to record the answers to these questions, adapting them to your circumstance. For instance: if you're a writer, you will need to determine how to publish; if you're an artist or musician, you will need space in which to show or perform your work. So:

- What kind of staff will you need to get your project off-the-ground?

- What is the order of project activities, and what financial resources do they require?

- What physical, or virtual, space and equipment will you need?

- How will you get the word out?

On the next page, I've given you an idea of how I've approached the organizing phase of my project.

Imagine:
- I've imagined several ways I want my story to be Herstory, but my first project is to create a women's center for my rural Michigan township

Create:
- *Who:* the women and girls of Keeler township

- *What:* a women's center where they can get help with childcare, finding a job, and furthering their education; and where they can gather together for celebrations and community service projects, including gathering with the community's girls to help them get the support they need and succeed in achieving their dreams

- *When:* in 2023

- *Where:* in a space near the town hall and fire station so that the center is accessible and has access to donated space

- *Why:* there are almost 1,000 households in the township where the median income for women is only $26,000; 20% of the children in these households live below the poverty line; only a third of the adult population has a two-year or four-year degree

Organize:
- Description of my start-up infrastructure: a donated room with an open space for gatherings, movable desks, and some computers

- My initial budget includes the cost of one part-time staffer paid contractually; and donated tech support, equipment and supplies

- Here is how I will connect with the community: I will reach out to inform and include every woman and girl in the township

When you organize a Herstory project, odds are you will experience opposition. For deeply-rooted sexism still exists. While the existence of sexism is likely the reason you have decided to do this work in the first place, you'll still need fortitude even once you've committed to work for justice. This poster's message aptly captures this truth. I also don't think we need to be concerned about what the equivalent female-gendered expression would be. If you've worked successfully in a male-dominated work setting, or supervised male employees, or, even, ever spoke up when you weren't supposed to, you may have been told you "have balls." I know I was. So be it. Let's apply this expression of our strength and fortitude to making Herstory, including for women who can't speak up or speak out but deserve the same justice.

- While organizing your project, think about the steps along the way that will require particular courage and how you will approach them. Outline some of those plans here for the project you've decided to work on, in light of the truth that Your Story as Herstory includes the downs as well as the ups.

- Since you'll be collaborating with others to realize your dream, are there ways you can teach them about how to manage confrontation? If so, note those here.

SOMETIMES
IT TAKES
bALLS
TO bE A
WOMAN

It's inevitable that while you are organizing, you will be asked to compromise; even to water down the project you've imagined and are now prepared to organize. You have the absolute right, as well as the responsibility, to determine whether the compromise you're being asked to make is sensible, or not. So, while your constant commitment is to "fight for what's right," the shape, even some of the substance, of your project may change if you decide the compromise you're asked to make makes sense. If you do compromise, remember that some of the greatest women activists adeptly modified their organizing strategies, still achieving great success. A recent example is what happened once it was clear that none of the 2020 Democratic women presidential candidates would be nominated to run for POTUS. So, we shifted the project to advocating for a woman vice-presidential candidate. We had to keep fighting for what's right: representation of women at the highest levels of government, in executive offices in particular, even if the progress would be slower than we'd hoped. Kamala Harris is now meeting with heads-of-state in the name of the US. Not a bad year's work!

- If you are asked to modify your organizing plan, remember to state your response in as compelling and definitive language as possible. In order to be prepared for this possibility, create a list here of the components of your organizing plan you think will face resistance, and how you will address this resistance.

- Treasure the moments of joy your fight for what's right will bring you! Don't forget to record those moments here and to share your joy with others.

_____

_____

_____

_____

_____

_____

_____

_____

_____

_____

_____

_____

_____

_____

_____

_____

_____

_____

_____

A truth of organizing for social justice is that it's possible to become self-righteous; to believe that the only truth is your truth and, therefore, not respect the existence of your opposition. But that's not wise. No one is infallible. There is, almost always, more than one way to achieve a good and just end. That's where "respect existence" comes in. This idea doesn't mean respecting reprehensible views or hate-filled actions, but it does mean respecting allies who have alternate strategies for achieving common goals. You may also "expect resistance" from those, unlike you, who haven't found a way to compromise when that is the wisest course. Remaining positive will be key to maintaining your commitment to continue organizing. So, I recommend thinking about these twists and turns along your path as *surmountable* obstacles; obstacles that will impel a feeling of accomplishment once you've addressed them.

- Even in the midst of strife, you can achieve a feeling of peacefulness once you've chosen to respect existence. "Let she who is without sin cast the first stone." Note here some of the ways you will share with those who disagree with you your commitment to respecting existence while finding a way forward.

- It's always smart when organizing to anticipate resistance. Think about the elements of your project and where you may experience resistance; then, about how you will overcome them.

_____

_____

_____   RESPECT
                                        EXISTENCE
_____   or
                                        EXPECT
_____   RESISTANCE

_____

_____

_____

_____

_____

_____

_____

_____

_____

_____

"What the fuck?"—women desperately need to move together forward! No beating-around-that-bush. However, digging deeper into "together forward" encompasses a lot of positive organizing activities. At the same time, as you collaborate with other women, will "together forward" require consensus before moving forward or a majority vote to determine how to proceed? Or some other decision making mechanism? Will "together forward" be conditioned on having built a diverse group of partners, or a group in which every woman will have a chance to lead? Will "together forward" be an ongoing partnership once your project is completed? And, for the artists, musicians, and athletes among you, remember that "women together forward" is an incredibly powerful rhetorical and audience-building context for Your Story as Herstory.

- The idea of "WTF" can be a useful expression of dismay when you feel fed up with your project organizing. But that doesn't mean giving up! It does mean taking the measure of the situation; discussing it with your project colleagues; and then proceeding in your organizing, having revamped as was needed. Record here the kinds of circumstances that will likely generate a "WTF" so that you can be prepared.

- Some of the women you partner with won't like the expression, "WTF." So, list here the words or phrases you could use instead to accurately reflect your dismay *with them.*

Women
Together
Forward

We are all equally-gifted, albeit in different ways. So, when you think about the phrase, "make America smart again," think about the many different ways in which "smart" can be envisioned and stated as an organizing goal for Your Story as Herstory. Don't fall into the trap of thinking there is only one way to be smart. For there isn't. Some women are smart at creating beauty—say, in art, or gardens, or music. Others are smart at making everyone feel welcome and part of the group. Another group of women is gifted at caring and mediating when there are differences that need to be resolved. Some women are smart because they are well-educated and keep learning. And yet another group of women is smart because they seem to be natural-born leaders and gifted advocates. For organizing your project, you will want to engage all of these types of smart women in making America smart again.

- Organizing an array of types of equally smart women is a big deal. Think here about the sequence of your organizing tasks. Does the nature of your project suggest a certain order of organizing all the smart women you want to engage with it?

- Think about whether you could "cross-train" your project's women so that all these smart women can learn from one another. How cool would that be?

DATE: /   /

MAKE
AMERICA
SMART
AGAIN

There is so much wisdom in this quote from Justice Ginsburg. Why shouldn't women be as prevalent in positions of power as men are—and have been–for centuries! In this context, remember that the US Supreme Court was all-male from 1790 to 1981: 191 years. If the US Supreme Court had only women members, it could remain that way for 191 years, and only then would parity be achieved. Some say we're getting there and are okay with that: three women justices in 2022—151 years after the first American woman became a lawyer. As you can see, Justice Ginsburg said "phooey" to this idea. I imagine she thought there was no rationale for sufficient US Supreme Court representation being modest for everyone but white men. To this point, Justice Ginsburg said, in her eminently pithy way: "I say, 'when there are nine [women],' people are shocked. But there'd been nine men, and nobody's ever raised a question about that."

- In your organizing, think about how you can engage as many women as possible in every aspect of the project. And, if you want to do like Justice Ginsburg said—and why not?—hire only women and only accept women volunteers.

- As you do your project organizing, think about the importance of publicizing your commitment to working with women and increasing their presence in jobs that have previously been predominantly held by men. This decision of yours is a wonderful one. Like Justice Ginsburg, you can share your commitment to women's equality everywhere as you make Your Story Herstory.

**HOW MANY
WOMEN
SHOULD BE
ON THE
SUPREME
COURT ?**

RBG: 9!

arlier, I wrote here about not going back to the 1950s. Well, there's also no reason to go back to the 1970s, or even the 1980s. By way of example, it was only in the 1970s when the US Supreme Court ruled that it was unconstitutional for a state to prohibit women serving on juries and that denying husbands military benefits was sex discrimination (thank you, Justice Ginsburg). It wasn't until the 1980s that the US Supreme Court held "[denying admission to men to university nursing programs] lends credibility to the old view that women, not men, should become nurses, and makes the assumption that nursing is a field for women a self-fulfilling prophecy." This was Justice O'Connor in her first US Supreme Court opinion. And, it took the Second Wave feminism of the 1970s and 1980s to revolutionize American women's lives in myriad ways: access to credit; expanding access to reproductive health services; guaranteeing women's equal opportunity in education due to the passage of Title IX: "No person in the United States shall, on the basis of sex, be excluded from participation in, be denied the benefits of, or be subjected to discrimination under any education program or activity receiving Federal financial assistance." Well, you get the picture: "Not Going Back."

- Your Story as Herstory can be revolutionary, too. Note here some ideas for how it can be.

- If there are elements of your project's organizing plan that risk being backwards in their view of success, e.g., failing to commit to leadership diversity, note here the ways in which you will organize to avoid such deficiencies. For instance, to avoid this circumstance, the project will create an aggressive affirmative action plan.

NOT GOING BACK

❚❚Power corrupts, and absolute power corrupts absolutely."
Back-in-the-day, I learned this truth. I've never forgotten
it. Subsequently, I have occasionally observed political
and social change project leaders (mostly white men)
who acted as though they had absolute power, to which
they had a right. That their patriarchy was oh, just fine.
Too many of them got away with this behavior because
others were scared to contest their assertion of power.
While "patriarchy" doesn't inevitably lead to corruption,
and there are plenty of men who consider themselves
patriarchs in family settings, who aren't corrupt and have
no public power, that other kind does deserve to have its
patriarchy smashed. For patriarchy has yielded structural
sex discrimination of the most profound and long-lasting
sort. For instance, the Equal Rights Amendment has still
not been fully ratified. Proposed in 1923 and passed by the
US Congress in 1972, it states: "Equality of rights under the
law shall not be denied or abridged by the United States or
by any state on account of sex." In 2021, not even a third
(30.9%) of state legislators are women. *Just imagine if the
patriarchy were smashed and those legislatures were 70%
women.*

- To "smash" in this context doesn't require being
  violent or destructive. It does mean to act forcefully
  and dispositively. How can you organize your project
  so that it is forceful and dispositive, when patriarchal
  actions rear their ugly heads?

- You'll need to be prepared for those who accuse you
  of wanting to replace patriarchy with matriarchy and
  claim that's an equally bad idea. You'll want to counter
  this argument forcefully and dispositively. You'll want
  to note some talking points here.

DATE: / /

THE PATRIARCHY AIN'T GONNA SMASH ITSELF

Michelle Obama remains—fifteen years after the world met her when Barack Obama first ran for POTUS—an inspirational figure. And that's because she not only says, "time to get to work"; she gets to work and inspires with her words of encouragement while doing so. I've never seen her be angry or impatient, even in trying circumstances, while experiencing backlash, or even while hatred is directed at her. As she says, and pointedly reminds us: "when they go low, we go high." As she goes high, she bears in mind this oft-repeated mantra of hers: "Be focused. Be determined. Be hopeful. Be empowered. Empower yourselves with a good education, then get out there and use that education to build a country worthy of your boundless promise. Lead by example with hope, never fear." Time to get to work.

- To "lead by example with hope" suggests that you, too, organize your project with generosity towards others. Think about the ways in which you will express this leadership approach.

- I think Michelle Obama would tell you (or any other woman) that your education for making the world a better place will take place in a variety of contexts, not just in a classroom. Think about what those contexts are for Your Story as Herstory, and how you can share them with other women who have the same dreams of leadership and willingness to work to achieve it as you do.

Time To Get To Work!

❚❚ I am here with the strength of thousands. Don't underestimate me. HERE TO STAY!" I love all three of the ideas expressed here: to be together with thousands in the march to justice (like the other graphics in this journal, this is a Women's March poster); don't ever underestimate me (note bold, all caps and big type so you don't miss the point!); and I'm here; not going anywhere (until this work is done). What better guidance for your organizing? This poster-maker's notion of togetherness is exactly right: a constant must, no matter what your project is. Some women think they can go it alone, or that they have all the bright ideas needed to organize a project, but I'm here to tell you they are mistaken. "No woman is an island," especially when it comes to her making Herstory, even Your Story as Herstory.

- How can you organize your project so that you keep enlarging the circle of those involved? Remember in this context that being at one with thousands doesn't have to be in-person; importantly, it can be in-spirit, too.

- When I was coming of age as a feminist, there was a lot of talk about women's "fear of success," even among those who sought to lead or do public projects like the one you're organizing. Earlier, in high school, we were told we would scare off the boys if we raised our hands in class! And that having a boyfriend, much less a husband, required this subservience! Of course, some women still suffer from fear of success. As you organize, what are the ways you will help your women partners who may have these feelings to overcome them so the project, you, and they can all flourish.

Estoy aquí con LA FUERZA de MILES de personas. NO me SUBESTIMES

Hectoslayl   B.C.

Often, when we think about American resistance to injustice, we think about women leaders of times past: Sojourner Truth, Mother Jones, Rosa Parks, or Pocahontas. But, as this image of Carrie Fisher as Princess Leia created by artist Hayley Gilmore declares, all of us—no matter our other roles or responsibilities—have a place in "The Resistance." Here is how Hayley described her creation of this image in an article in the newspaper of her hometown, Columbus, Mississippi: "To me, Carrie Fisher's portrayal of Princess Leia is one that really resonates with, not only me, but a lot of women. Because she's strong, intelligent, sassy. She doesn't wait to be rescued. She goes in headfirst." As you're organizing, I recommend Hayley's idea to you: dive in headfirst and keep on swimming.

- Whether your project is a service, artistic, or political one, and even if not politically combative, in creating and organizing Your Story as Herstory, you are resisting norms that prevent women from realizing their freedoms, just like those heroes of decades gone by did. What are the organizing strategies you will use to make your project a part of The Resistance as well as an inspirational one?

- I'm thinking of The Resistance as a circle every woman can join and thus be on an equal footing with every other woman in the circle. This is a powerful image for your organizing. How can you use it in telling Your Story as Herstory, one in which the sisterhood is powerful and equal?

WOMAN'S
PLACE
IS IN
THE
RESISTANCE

Since we all belong to The Resistance, we are also all in this together. This poster-maker reinforced her view of this truth by encircling the message with various significant images. I see the US flag, the gay pride flag in the lower left corner and the symbols for peace and equality. It seems to me her notion was that we are in this together, regardless. This sign was also quite large; perhaps, ten feet wide. Clearly, its creator (creators?) wanted to make sure marchers didn't miss it. Also, shouting this belief to the proverbial rooftops above that marchers' street strikes me as just the best idea.

- As you're organizing your project, how will you shout to the rooftops your belief that we are all in this together? How many different ways can you imagine this joyous shouting?

- When you commit to being together to make Herstory, it's still likely there will be disagreements from time-to-time about how to move forward. What are your regrouping strategies?

WE ARE IN THIS TOGETHER

Hear us holler about the myriad ways in which income inequality hurts every woman and her family. Think about it: fewer dollars to save for a rainy day, buy a home, go to college, send a child to camp, or even just to buy groceries. If she, or you, want to financially support women candidates or causes benefiting women, this discrimination hurts again. Think about it: for every dollar a man has earned and can give, you will have earned 78 cents (or less, if you are a woman of color) you could give. And this calculation includes the dollars you've earned and saved to fund your startup project, making Your Story Herstory.

- What are your ideas for public information and outreach campaigns that promote elimination of this systemic inequality that could complement your project's plan?

- How will you incorporate into your project's fundraising plan the idea that, due to this wage inequity, those with the means to do so should give even more than they might have thought to—in this way helping to make up for the inequity?

Same pencils
Same exams
Hear us holler
Same scores
Same careers
78 Cents to
his dollar

But we can handle it. Alas, there is no getting around it: those who oppose women will, as they have done throughout *history*, prevent women from rising up, working for equal justice, or fighting to make Herstory. I'm going to make an exception here to quote a man I admire, Congressman Hakeem Jeffries: "a knockout is not a knock down." Nastiness doesn't have to win. The district he represents includes many of the same Brooklyn (New York) neighborhoods that Shirley Chisholm (the first African American woman Member of Congress) represented. In a speech he gave, Congressman Jeffries spoke of Chisholm's influence on him: "[Jeffries] imagines her voice in his head, he said, telling him, 'We sent you down to Washington to stand up, so don't go down there and act up.'" Jeffries imagines Chisholm reminding him there would be foolishness and nastiness, *but so what!* Your duty is constant: in order to make Your Story as Herstory, stand up— and fight like a girl.

- I imagine Chisholm also calling on us to stand up for one another, though I don't know she ever said these words: "When the night has come/And the land is dark/ And the moon is the only light we'll see/No, I won't be afraid/Oh, I won't be afraid/Just as long as you stand/ Stand by me." Another New Yorker, soul singer Ben E. King, wrote (with Jerry Leiber and Mike Stoller) and first sang these words in the song, "Stand by Me." It has been covered by over 400 other singers, including John Lennon, Tina Turner, U2, Bono, Bruce Springsteen, and country western singers Mickey Gilley and Ronnie Milsap. What does that tell you? *"Stand by me" is a plea from each of us to the rest of us. When there is nastiness, have no fear.* Record here (pun intended) how you will promulgate this message in your project's work.

- How will you avoid being nasty yourself? The end of your project is in sight, and you don't want to diminish it in any way, and never in this way.

_____

_____

_____

_____   **THE**
                                                    FUTURE
_____   **IS**
                                                    NASTY
_____

_____

_____

_____

_____

_____

_____

_____

_____

_____

_____

_____

W e need to elect the first woman US president as soon as possible....*Yes, SHE can."*

I wrote these words in the Introduction to my book, *Vote Her In: Your Guide to Electing Our First Woman President*, published when millions of us hoped that first woman POTUS would be elected in 2020. While we were right in imagining that this victory would make Herstory by demonstrating that there is nothing women can't do, that was not to be proven in 2020.

However, as you know, we did get closer to seeing a woman behind the desk in the Oval Office than ever before. Yes, SHE did. Kamala Harris made *her story*. American troops salute her. Women and girls all over the world see her, a woman of color, in one of the most important jobs in the world. American women know, in a way they didn't before, the glorious future we can create for each other when we come together to create and organize. Now, with the daily inspiration that Kamala Harris's presence in the Oval Office provides, you can keep making Herstory for *every woman*; by realizing Your Story as Herstory, *your* dreams of justice every day for every other woman can happen, too.

I know you're well-prepared for this journey: you've imagined, created, organized, and recorded your making Herstory projects here. You've examined yourself and realized–and celebrated–the strength, discipline, intelligence, and care you possess—and are willing to share with others.

I opened this journal by sharing the story of women who made Herstory one hundred years ago, whose own vivid imaginings led to revolutionary organizing to improve the lives of women and girls. Fifty years ago, the word "Herstory" was first used in print in the book, *Sisterhood Is Powerful.* Now, it's your turn for *Your Story* to be *Herstory.*

My description of the project I've imagined, created, and organized:

_____

_____

_____

_____

_____

_____

_____

_____

_____

_____

_____

_____

_____

_____

_____

My notes about other ideas and projects that keep coming to mind

I'M A FEMINIST
What's YOUR
SUPERPOWER?

Rebecca's Word Alphabet to Inspire Your Story as Herstory

Agitate

Bold

Clamor

Define

Excel

Follow

Galvanize

Help

Initiate

Joy

Keep

Leader

Move

Nation

Organize

Politics

Query

Resist

Solve

Trust

Understand

Volunteer

Wonder

X(e)xcel

Your

Zest

Organizations I want to join and support

- _____
  _____
  _____
  _____

- _____
  _____
  _____
  _____

- _____
  _____
  _____
  _____

- _____
  _____
  _____
  _____

Women's stories
and movements
I want to learn
about

**WE ARE
WOMEN
HEAR US**

ROAR

- _____
  _____

- _____
  _____

- _____
  _____

- _____
  _____

- _____
  _____

- _____
  _____

- _____
  _____

- _____

Inspirational quotes I have run across

Here's one to get you started:

> **"Nobody's free until everybody's free."**
> **Fannie Lou Hamer**
> Civil rights activist, farmer

- _____
  _____
  _____

- _____
  _____
  _____

- _____
  _____
  _____

- _____
  _____
  _____

Notes to myself

Take some time to complete this page however you like. Perhaps, some of the words in Rebecca's Alphabet will inspire you.

Here are some categories of notes:

- Messages to your girlfriends
- Links you want to share
- Photos you want to find
- Music you want to listen to
- Books you want to read
- Your athletic goals

"Give light and people will find the way."

Ella Baker

Civil rights and human rights activist

"There is still...so much history to be made."

Michelle Obama

First Lady, lawyer, women's rights activist, author

"There is nothing more powerful than a group of determined sisters marching alongside their determined sons, brothers, fathers, and friends standing up for what we know is right."

The Hon. Kamala Harris
Vice President, lawyer, and former U.S. Senator

Rebecca Sive is the author of two prior books on women, politics, and power: *Every Day Is Election Day: A Woman's Guide to Winning Any Office, from the PTA to the White House*, and *Vote Her In: Your Guide to Electing Our First Woman President*, and many articles. Since the 1970s, she has been a feminist movement leader and community organizer. An inspirational public speaker, former public official, including as a commissioner of the Illinois Human Rights Commission, leader of the movement to elect Chicago's first Black mayor (Harold Washington), and advisor to numerous women candidates and officials, she is a past lecturer at the Harris School of Public Policy at the University of Chicago. Sive holds an M.A. in American History and is the recipient of many awards for her public leadership. She is a collector of women's art and women's movement ephemera.

Sive may be found at www.rebeccasive.com.

"As a strategist for women leaders, I share with you this immutable truth: every woman I've met has made her own herstory. You can, too, with the new journal, *Make Herstory Your Story* – it's for every woman everywhere reaching for the stars."

Celinda Lake
Pollster, Joe Biden, POTUS
Founder, Lake Research Partners

"Barack Obama (my boss) gave me—and millions of other Black women—the opportunity to lead. Rebecca Sive (my professor) has given all of us *Make Herstory Your Story*, a personal journal for getting the job done."

Alexandra P. Sims
Field Director for Obama 2012
Founder, Black Bench Chicago
Founder, Every Vote Counts

"*Make Herstory Your Story* is the perfect journal for every woman who aspires to lead and make the world a better place. Time to record your dreams and make your plans! Heartfelt thanks to my friend Rebecca for this beautiful gift for all of us."

The Hon. Jan Schakowsky
Member, US House of Representatives

"Women are so often the engines of democracy, social change, and community care. In *Make Herstory Your Story*, Rebecca Sive, an accomplished organizer and activist, offers a guided journal with inspiration and encouragement. It's fuel for the important work ahead."

Anna Galland
National organizer and strategist
Former Executive Director, MoveOn Civic Action

"What a brilliant invitation to ponder our connections to the women who came before us, the women with whom we share this moment, and the women for whom we're shaping the world—and then turn that pondering into sustainable, impactful change."

Heidi Stevens
Journalist and Parent Nation creative director

"*Make Herstory Your Story* is the perfect journal for every woman and girl with big dreams and plans for a better world. I wish I had had it when I was growing up!"

The Hon. Anna Valencia
Chicago City Clerk

"Rebecca Sive's new journal for women activists with big dreams, *Make Herstory Your Story*, is an inspirational and indispensable resource for us all. Our personal stories are an important part of what defines us as leaders and telling our story helps us connect with others."

The Hon. Dana Nessel
Attorney General, State of Michigan

"My friend Rebecca's inspirational new book—the journal, *Make Herstory Your Story*—is a must-have for every woman committed to bending the arc towards justice."

The Hon. Dr. Robin Kelly
Chair, Illinois Democratic Party

"The *Make Herstory Your Story* journal for aspiring women leaders is a terrific resource. It will motivate and inspire you to start your journey now, to which I say: 'welcome.'"

Jill Wine-Banks
Author, *The Watergate Girl: My Fight for Truth and Justice Against a Criminal President*
Legal Analyst and Co-host, #SistersInLaw podcast

"*Make Herstory Your Story* is a wonderful guide for women who want to change the world and are looking for inspiration from those who have gone before them. If you're not sure where to start—but want to get going—*Make Herstory Your Story* is for you."

Heather Booth
Organizer
Founder, Midwest Academy

"*Make Herstory Your Story* imagines a world in which every woman has the power within her to create a more just world. It then gives us the encouragement to stretch our imaginations to become the leaders these trying times require."

Kathryn Kolbert
Co-author, *Controlling Women: What We Must Do Now to Save Reproductive Freedom*; reproductive rights activist

"*Make Herstory Your Story* encourages women to dream boundlessly—and makes action feel like an inevitability. It's easy to imagine future changemakers filling these pages with ambitious visions and outlines for a better world. Rebecca Sive wonderfully delivers the inspiration and the tools-to steer them across the finish line."

Jordan Zaslow
Founder, Her Bold Move

"What a great resource *Make Herstory Your Story* will be for young women leaders. I can't wait to share it."

The Hon. Sarah Godlewski
Wisconsin State Treasurer